How to Sparkle at

Beginning Multiplication and Division

Moira Wilson

Brilliant
PUBLICATIONS

We hope you and your class enjoy using this book. Other books in the series include:

To find out more details on any of our resources, please log onto our website:
www.brilliantpublications.co.uk.

Published by Brilliant Publications
Unit 10, Sparrow Hall Farm, Edlesborough, Dunstable, Bedfordshire, LU6 2ES, UK

E-mail: info@brilliantpublications.co.uk
Website: www.brilliantpublications.co.uk

General information enquiries:
Tel: 01525 222292

The name Brilliant Publications and the logo are registered trademarks.

Written by Moira Wilson
Illustrated by Moira Wilson

Printed in the UK.
First published in 1999. Reprinted 2009.
10 9 8 7 6 5 4 3 2

© Moira Wilson 1999
Printed ISBN 978 1 897675 30 4
ebook ISBN 978 0 85747 058 4

Contents

Introduction

This book contains an abundance of stimulating activity sheets and games that will enable children to develop a thorough understanding of early multiplication and division. Various aspects of multiplication and division are covered, these being outlined with their corresponding pages as indicated.

Repeated addition   Pages 6, 13, 19, 26 and 31 introduce multiplication as the addition of equal groups of objects.

Counting and grouping   Pages 7, 8, 14, 20, 27, 28 and 32 give children experience of working with equivalent sets and partitioning sets using 2s, 3s, 4s, 5s and 10s.

Multiples   Pages 9, 15, 21, 22, 25, 33 and 36 explore patterns of multiples and the relationship between them. For example, doubling multiples of 2 produces multiples of 4; halving multiples of 10 produces multiples of 5.

Sharing   Pages 10, 11, 16, 17, 23, 29 and 34 require children to share out equally between a given number of subsets.

Repeated subtraction   Pages 12, 18, 24, 30 and 35 require children to work out how many subsets there will be if the number in each subset is known.

Multiplication and division facts   Pages 37 to 48 provide opportunities for children to reinforce and consolidate their understanding of the operations of multiplication and division.

Links to the National Curriculum

Close reference has been made to the National Curriculum in the writing of this book. The activities relate to the following programmes of study for Key Stage 1:

Pupils should be given opportunities to:

Using and applying mathematics
2a   select and use the appropriate mathematics;
2b   select and use mathematical equipment and materials;
3d   use a variety of forms of mathematical presentation.

Number
3b   explore and record patterns of multiples, *eg 3, 6, 9, 12*, explaining their patterns and using them to make predictions; progress to exploring further patterns involving multiplication and division, including those within a hundred-square of multiplication facts;
3b   learn multiplication and division facts relating to the 2s, 5s and 10s and use these to learn other facts, *eg double multiples of 2 to produce multiples of 4*, and to develop mental methods for finding new results;
4b   understand the operations of multiplication, and division as sharing and repeated subtraction, and use them to solve problems with whole numbers.

Successful linking of the activities to the programme of study depends to some extent on the way they are presented to the children and subsequent adult input. The page entitled 'How to use this book' explores this in further detail.

How to use this book

The activity sheets in this book form an indispensable bank of ideas that can be used to supplement any core mathematics scheme. Although there is built-in progression, it is not essential that a child should complete every page or that the pages should be used in a certain order. Rather, the book is intended to be a 'dip-in' resource that you can use to give children support, practice or consolidation as and when you feel it is necessary.

Use of terminology 'multiplied by' or 'times'

As far as possible, use of this terminology has been restricted because some schemes favour 'x' to be read as 'multiplied by' whereas others favour it to be read as 'times'. For example, 3 x 5 read as '3 multiplied by 5' would be represented pictorially by 5 sets of 3 objects or 3 + 3 + 3 + 3 + 3. However, 3 x 5 read as '3 times 5' would be represented pictorially by 3 sets of 5 objects or 5 + 5 + 5. The format of the book is such that 'x' has only been used where there is no pictorial representation. Therefore, either kind of terminology can be used.

Use of worksheets

The worksheets should always be preceded by practical work using real objects. For example:

Page 35   To introduce the idea of 'repeated subtraction'

* In a group session, ask 4 children to 'act out' the characters on the page and set tasks for the audience. You could give a child in the audience 12 marbles and say, 'Which of these actors can have 4 marbles each?'

* Gather together some yoghurt pots and a selection of counting objects. Arrange the children in groups and set them assorted tasks. For example, give them 4 marbles, 8 beads, 12 conkers, 16 pine cones and 20 cubes. Taking each type of object in turn, ask them to work out how many of the yoghurt pots can have 4 objects each.

Page 34   To introduce the idea of 'sharing equally'

* In a group session, ask 4 children to be actors again. Set tasks for the audience such as 'Share these 8 conkers equally amongst the 4 actors'.

* As for page 35, use counting objects but this time, only 4 yoghurt pots. Ask the children to share 4, 8, 12, 16 and 20 objects amongst the yoghurt pots.

You should then read through the instructions on the page and show the children examples of the required activity. When involved in the task, some children will benefit from further practical experience of moving objects into different groupings. It is also important to encourage them to use specific language associated with multiplication and division such as 'equal', 'equally', 'groups', 'lots', 'sets', 'share between' and 'share amongst'.

When completed and dated, the pages can be stored in the children's mathematical folders, creating a useful record of work covered.

Teddy bears

Count the ears on the teddy bears.

Continue this repeated addition pattern for 6, 7, 8, 9 and 10 teddy bears.

Balloons

Draw 2 balloons for each child.

Write the number of balloons in the boxes.

1 child has ☐ balloons.

2 children have ☐ balloons.

3 children have ☐ balloons.

4 children have ☐ balloons.

5 children have ☐ balloons.

Draw 5 more children, each with 2 balloons.

Write number sentences for 6, 7, 8, 9 and 10 children.

Mini-beasts

Draw a ring round each group of 2 mini-beasts.

☐ groups of 2

☐ group of 2

☐ groups of 2

☐ groups of 2

☐ groups of 2

Circus dots

Counting in twos, join the dots.

The numbers in the box are jumbled up.
Counting in twos, write them in order on the line below.

6		12		20	4
	10			16	
14		18	2		8

Feeding time

Share the food equally between each pair of creatures.

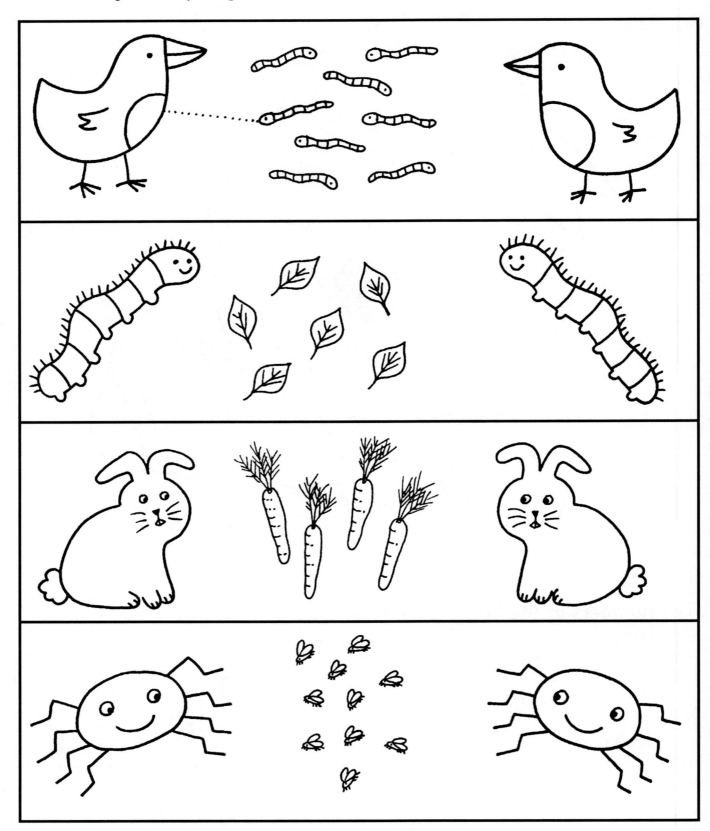

Marbles

Share the marbles equally between each pair of hands.

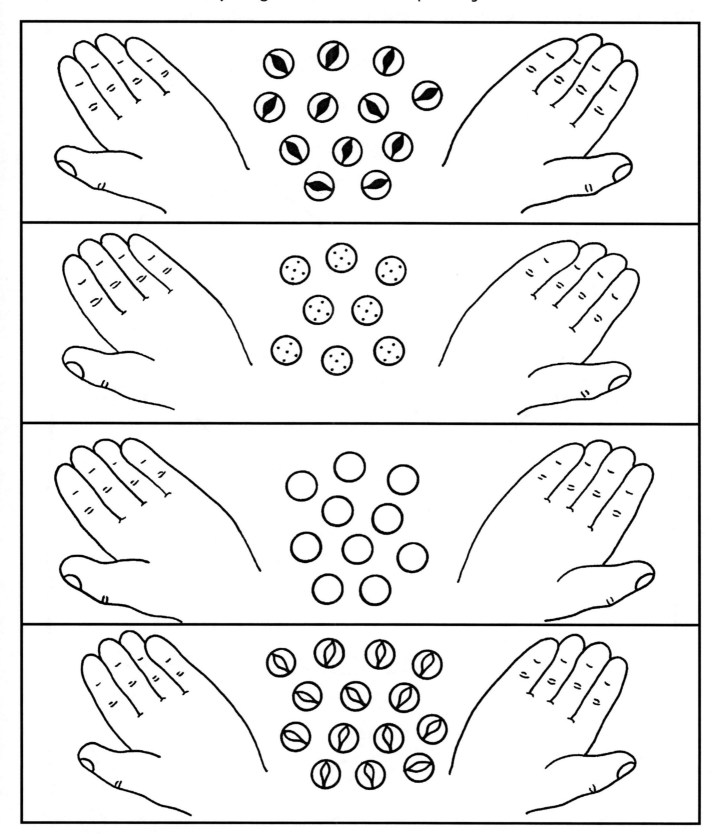

Sweet jars

Colour the sweets. Put 2 of each colour in as many jars as you can. You may not have enough of each colour for every jar.

green

red

black

orange

yellow

Snakes

Count the spots on the snakes.

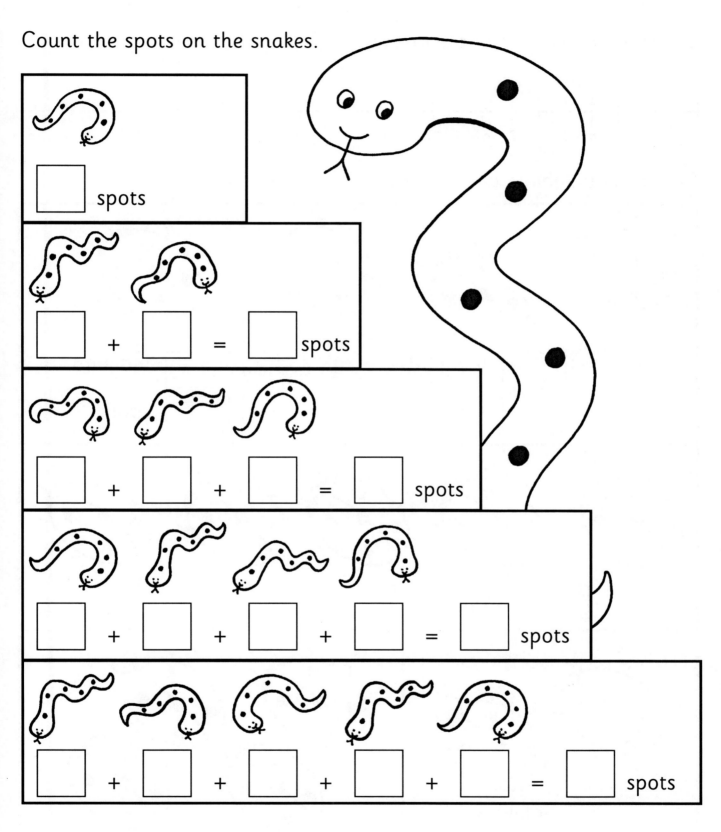

Continue this repeated addition pattern for 6, 7, 8, 9 and 10 snakes.

Ladybirds

Counting in fives, draw the arrows.

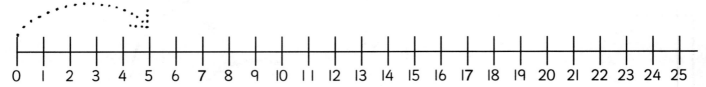

Count the ladybirds and the spots. Write the numbers.

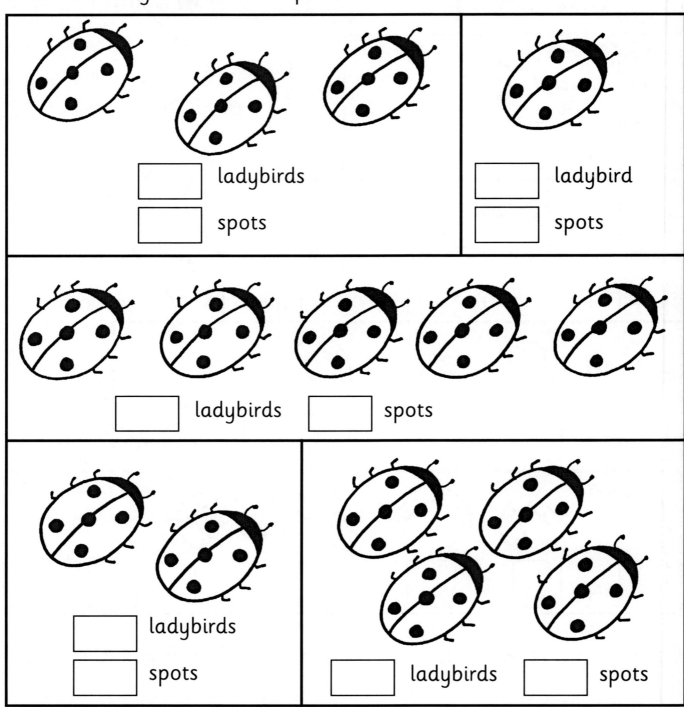

Dangerous dots

Counting in fives, join the dots.

The numbers in the box are jumbled up.
Counting in fives, write them in order on the line below.

25	50	15	45	20	
10	30	35	5	40	

Crackers

Share the decorations equally between 5. Draw them on the crackers.

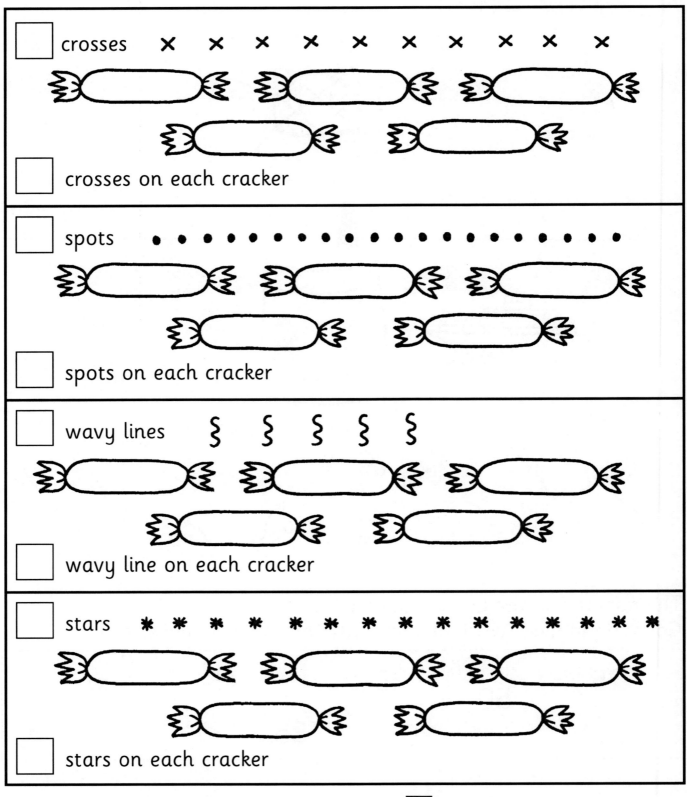

Draw 5 more crackers. Share 25 squares ■ equally between them.

Magic monsters

There are five monsters. Help the magician to share out the things in the star equally amongst them.

Draw
10 stripes
20 legs
5 noses
15 teeth
25 spots

Counters

Colour the counters. Put 5 of each colour in as many bags as you can. You may not have enough of each colour for every bag.

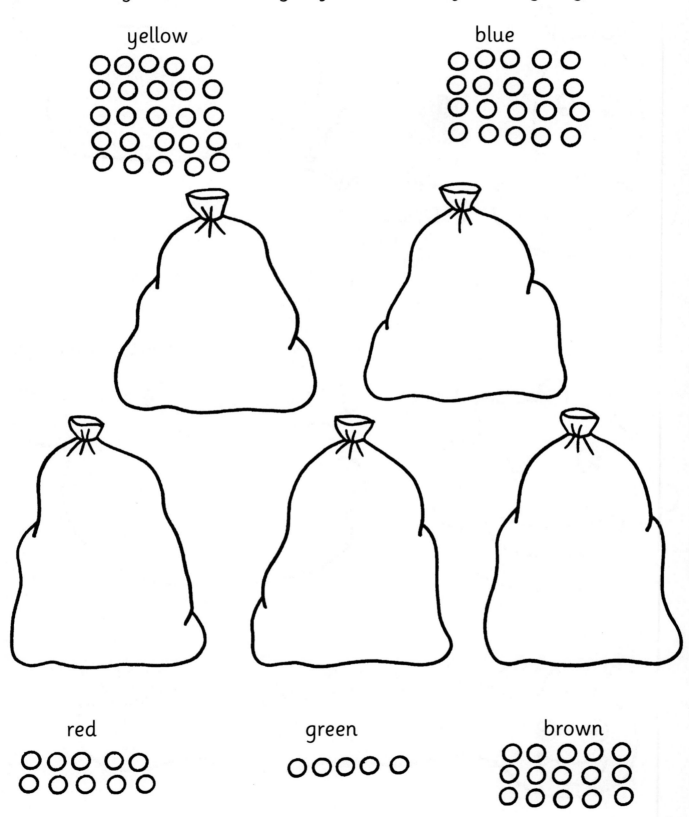

yellow

blue

red

green

brown

Clowns

Count the spots on the bow ties.

Continue this repeated addition pattern for 6, 7, 8, 9 and 10 bow ties.

How to Sparkle at Beginning Multiplication & Division
www.brilliantpublications.co.uk

Flowers

Write the number of petals in the boxes.

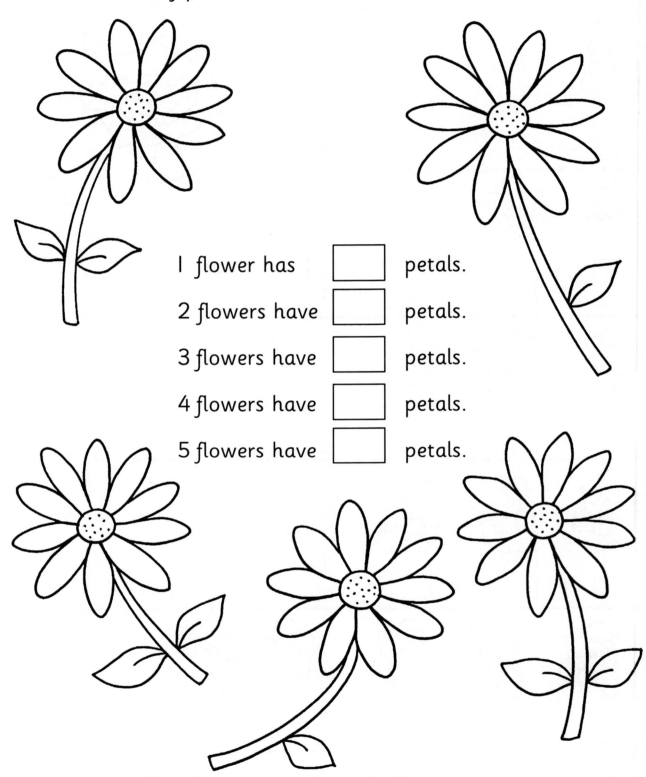

1 flower has ☐ petals.

2 flowers have ☐ petals.

3 flowers have ☐ petals.

4 flowers have ☐ petals.

5 flowers have ☐ petals.

Draw 5 more flowers, each with 10 petals.
Write number sentences for 6, 7, 8, 9 and 10 flowers.

Jumping frogs

Fred Frog can only count in fives. Draw blue circles round his numbers.

Flo Frog can only count in tens. Draw green circles round her numbers.

1	2	3	4	5	6	7	8	9	10
11	12	13	14	15	16	17	18	19	20
21	22	23	24	25	26	27	28	29	30
31	32	33	34	35	36	37	38	39	40
41	42	43	44	45	46	47	48	49	50
51	52	53	54	55	56	57	58	59	60
61	62	63	64	65	66	67	68	69	70
71	72	73	74	75	76	77	78	79	80
81	82	83	84	85	86	87	88	89	90
91	92	93	94	95	96	97	98	99	100

Fred

Flo

Write the missing numbers in Fred and Flo's lily pads.

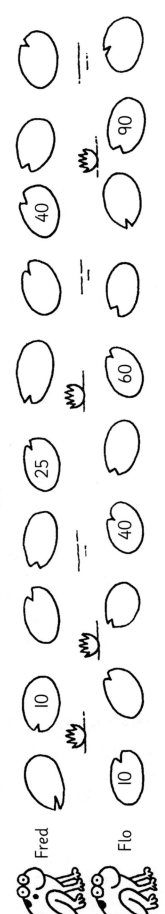

Fred

Flo

Space dots

Counting in tens, join the dots.

The numbers in the box are jumbled up.
Counting in tens, write them in order on the line below.

30		80		50	10
	60				
				70	
100		40	20		90

Creepy creatures

There are ten creatures. Help the magician to share out the things in the star equally amongst them.

Draw
40 spots
20 teeth
10 noses
30 legs
50 stripes

Dogs and bones

Count back to 0 in tens or fives along the paths to help the dogs get to the bones.

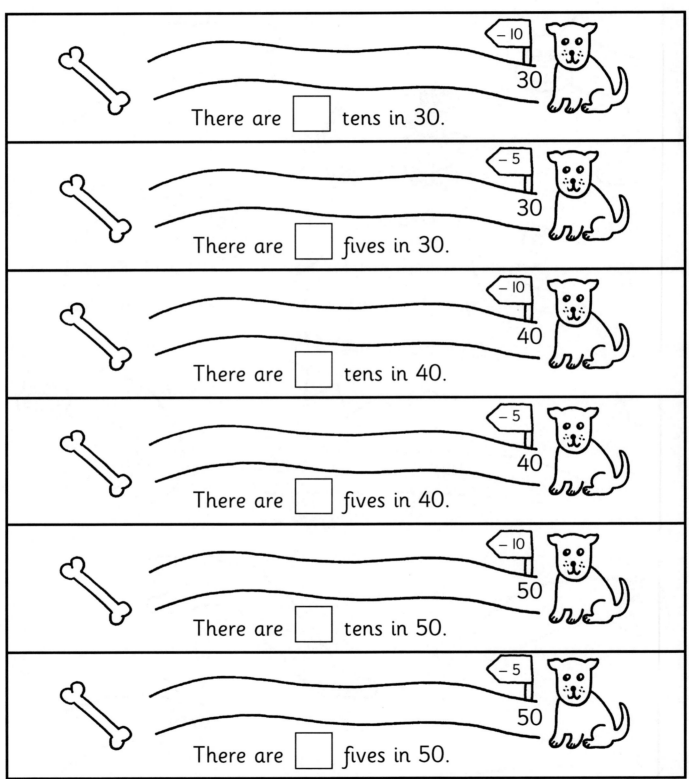

There are ☐ tens in 30.

There are ☐ fives in 30.

There are ☐ tens in 40.

There are ☐ fives in 40.

There are ☐ tens in 50.

There are ☐ fives in 50.

Write about any patterns you notice.

How to Sparkle at Beginning Multiplication & Division
24   www.brilliantpublications.co.uk

It's raining

Use the secret raindrop code to colour the umbrellas.

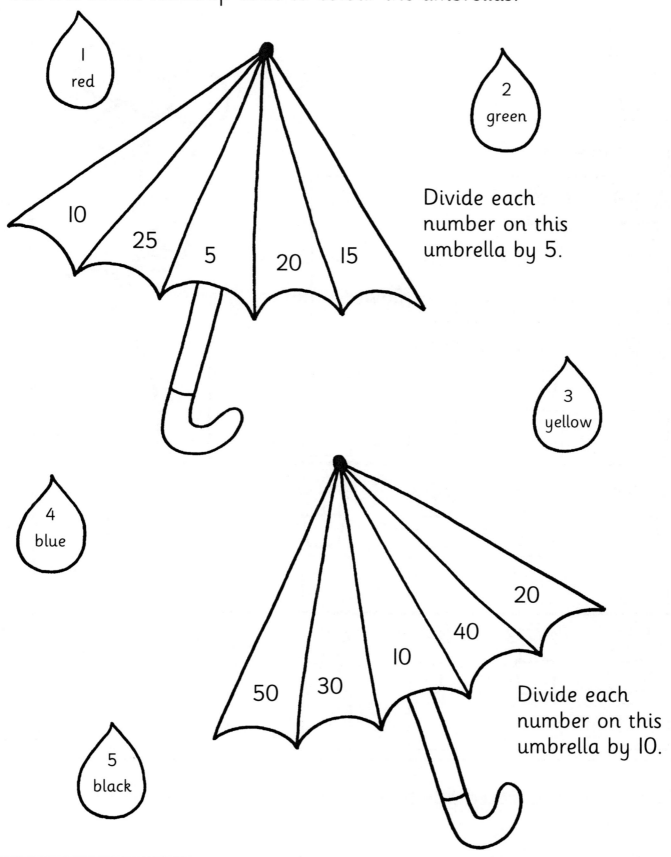

1 red

2 green

Divide each number on this umbrella by 5.

3 yellow

4 blue

5 black

Divide each number on this umbrella by 10.

Flower pots

Count the flowers.

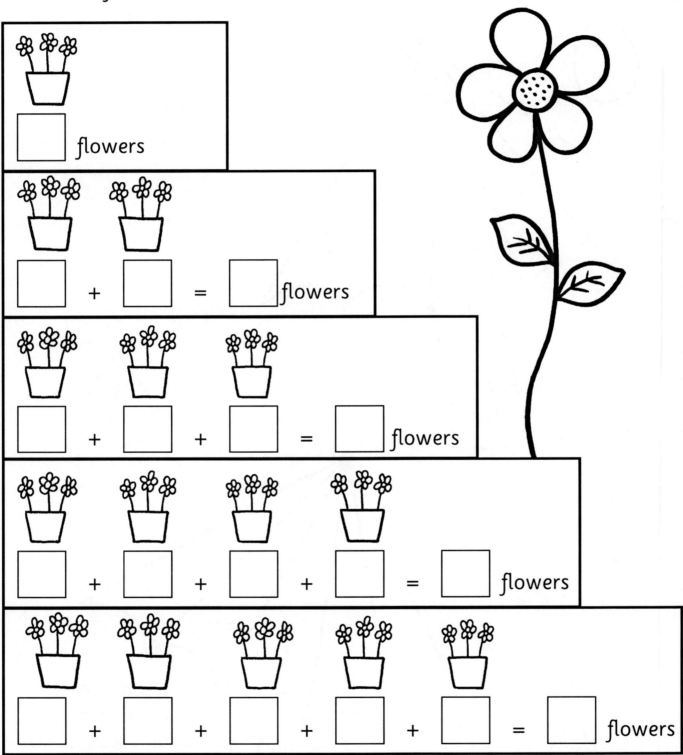

Continue this repeated addition pattern for 6, 7, 8, 9 and 10 flower pots.

Spotty fish

Write the numbers in the boxes.

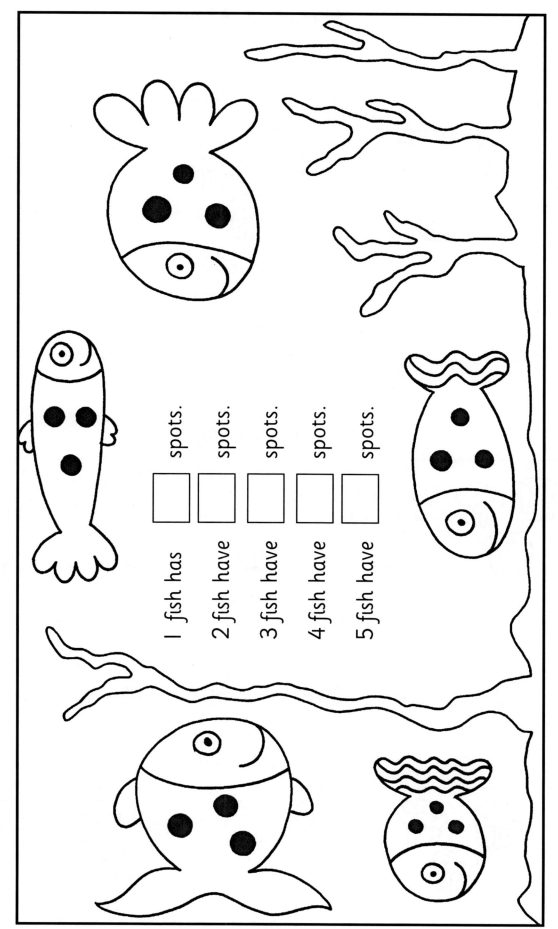

1 fish has ☐ spots.

2 fish have ☐ spots.

3 fish have ☐ spots.

4 fish have ☐ spots.

5 fish have ☐ spots.

Draw 5 more fish, each with 3 spots. Write number sentences for 6, 7, 8, 9 and 10 fish.

Party time

Draw a ring round each group of 3 cakes.

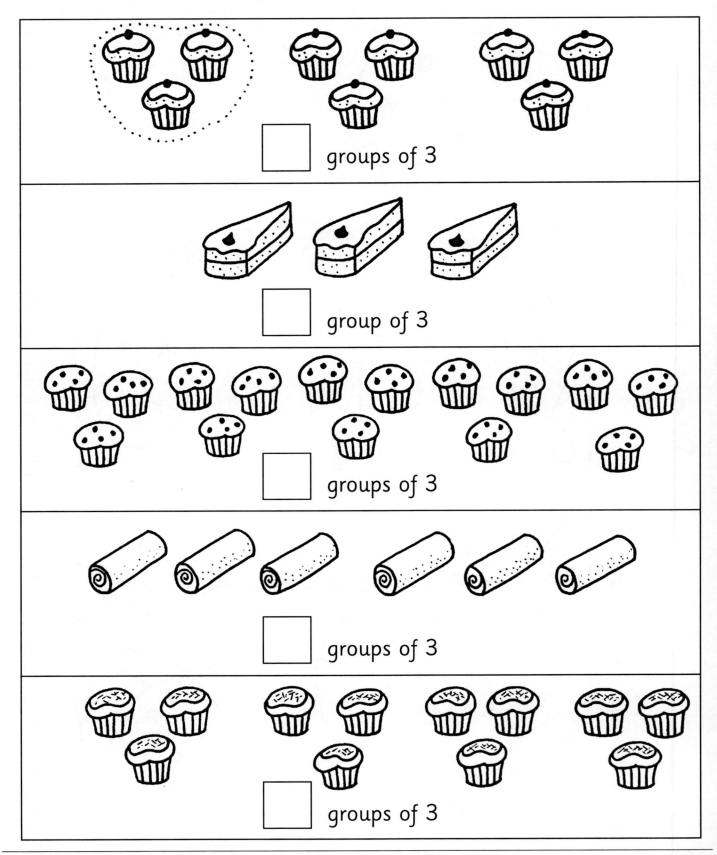

☐ groups of 3

☐ group of 3

☐ groups of 3

☐ groups of 3

☐ groups of 3

Lots of fruit

Share the fruit equally between 3. Draw the fruit in the bags.

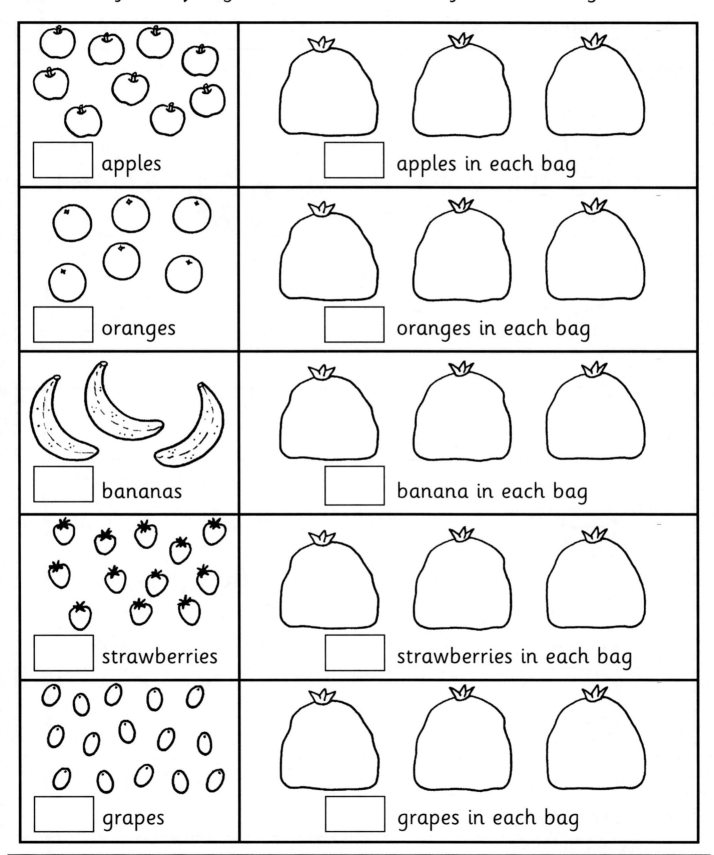

[ ] apples

[ ] apples in each bag

[ ] oranges

[ ] oranges in each bag

[ ] bananas

[ ] banana in each bag

[ ] strawberries

[ ] strawberries in each bag

[ ] grapes

[ ] grapes in each bag

Hungry dogs

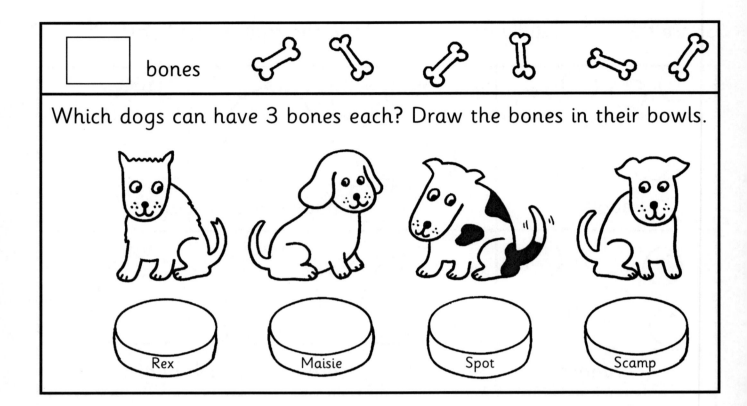

□ bones

Which dogs can have 3 bones each? Draw the bones in their bowls.

Rex   Maisie   Spot   Scamp

□ biscuits

Which dogs can have 3 biscuits each? Draw the biscuits in their bowls.

Rex   Maisie   Spot   Scamp

If you had 9 sausages ⬭ , which dogs could have 3 each?

Write their names: _____

Flags

Count the stars on the flags and write the numbers in the sandcastles.

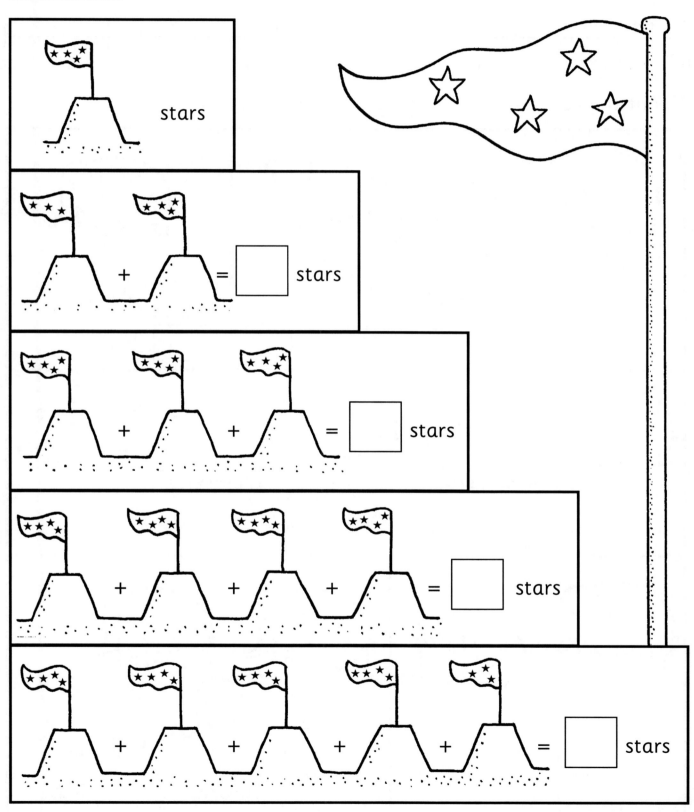

stars

+ = [ ] stars

+ + = [ ] stars

+ + + = [ ] stars

+ + + + = [ ] stars

Elephants

Counting in fours, draw the arrows.

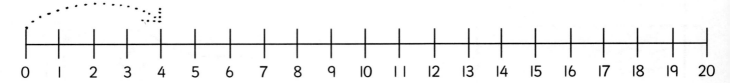

Count the elephants and the legs. Write the numbers.

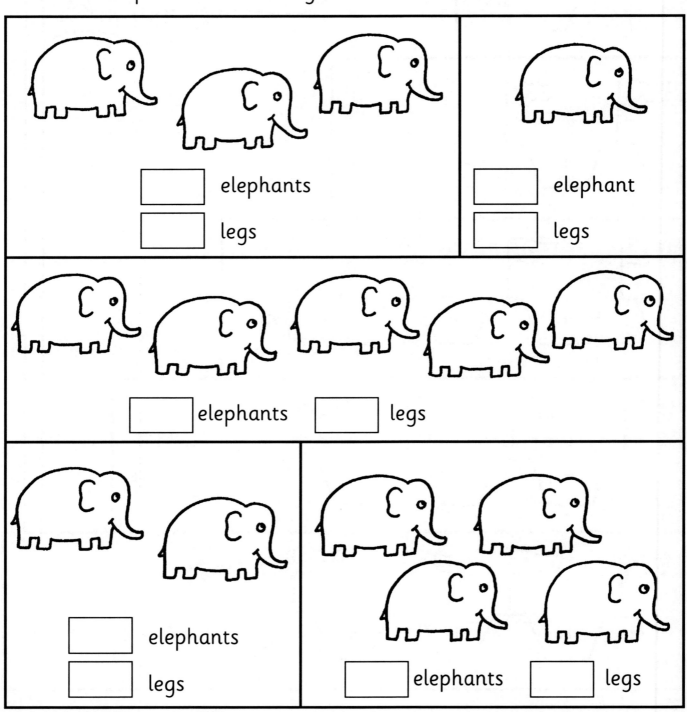

Bunny jumps

Roger Rabbit can only count in twos. Draw red circles round his numbers.

Rachel Rabbit can only count in fours. Draw blue circles round her numbers.

1	2	3	4	5	6	7	8	9	10
11	12	13	14	15	16	17	18	19	20
21	22	23	24	25	26	27	28	29	30
31	32	33	34	35	36	37	38	39	40
41	42	43	44	45	46	47	48	49	50
51	52	53	54	55	56	57	58	59	60
61	62	63	64	65	66	67	68	69	70
71	72	73	74	75	76	77	78	79	80
81	82	83	84	85	86	87	88	89	90
91	92	93	94	95	96	97	98	99	100

Roger

Rachel

Write the missing numbers in Roger and Rachel's holes.

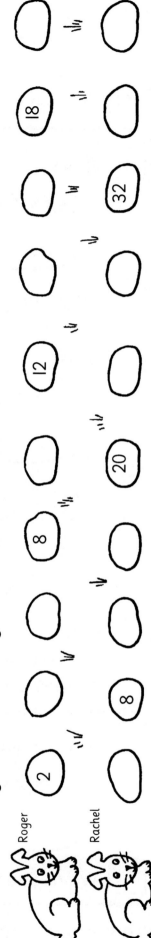

Roger

Rachel

Party hats

Share the decorations equally between 4. Draw them on the hats.

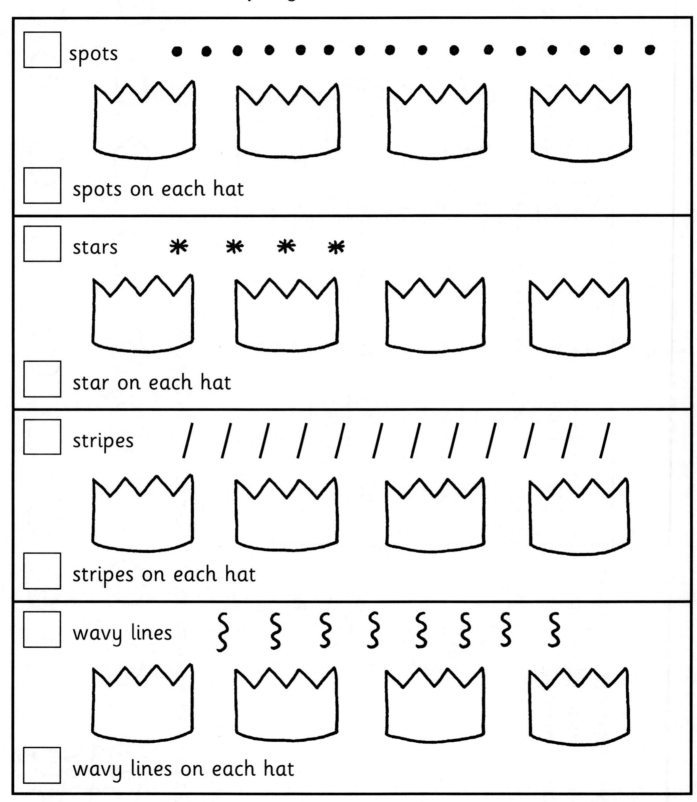

☐ spots •

☐ spots on each hat

☐ stars ✳ ✳ ✳ ✳

☐ star on each hat

☐ stripes / / / / / / / / / / / / /

☐ stripes on each hat

☐ wavy lines § § § § § § § §

☐ wavy lines on each hat

Draw 4 more hats. Share 20 triangles equally between them.

How to Sparkle at Beginning Multiplication & Division
www.brilliantpublications.co.uk

Hungry children

sweets

Which children can have 4 sweets each? Draw the sweets on their plates.

Millie   Jake   Tess   Freddie

lollipops

Which children can have 4 lollipops each? Draw the lollipops on their plates.

Millie   Jake   Tess   Freddie

If you had 16 cakes 🧁 , which children could have 4 each?

Write their names: _____

Tropical fish

Use the secret bubble code to colour the fish.

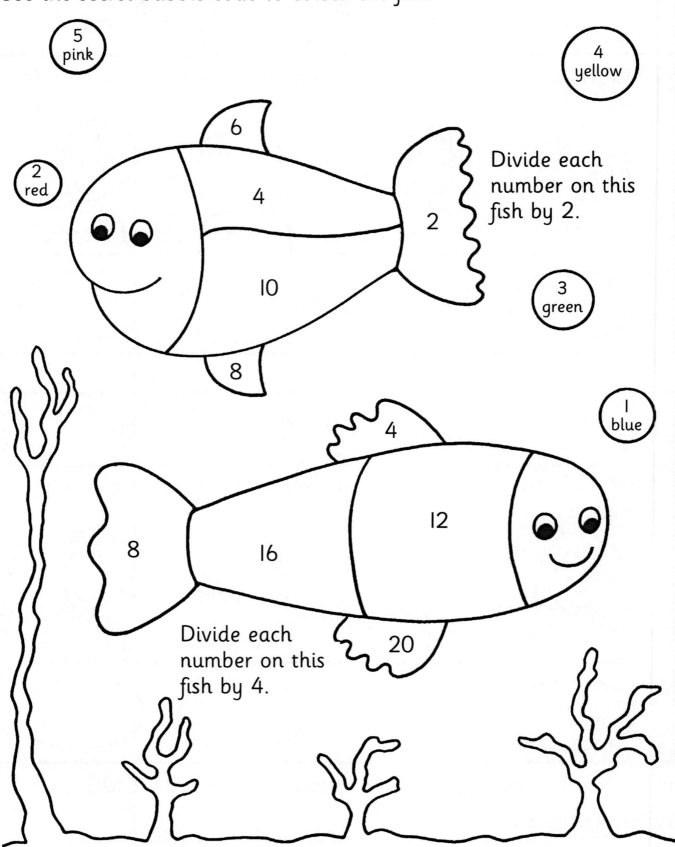

5 pink

4 yellow

2 red

6

4

2

10

8

Divide each number on this fish by 2.

3 green

1 blue

4

8

16

12

20

Divide each number on this fish by 4.

Where is my egg?

Draw a line from each hen to its egg.

3 x 2

4 x 4

5 x 3

20

10

6

15

10 x 2

2 x 5

16

30

9

3 x 4

5 x 5

8

12

25

10 x 3

2 x 4

3 x 3

Multiplication function machines

Write the missing numbers on each machine.

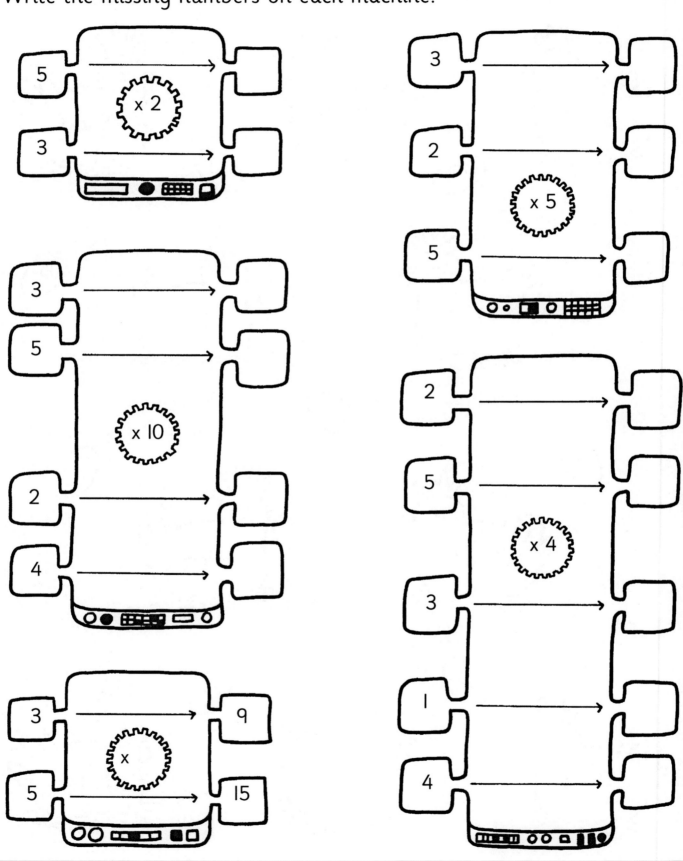

Multiplication Martians

Use the numbers in the box to make up your own sums.
Make each sum different.

2	10	3	5	4	1

Flower fun

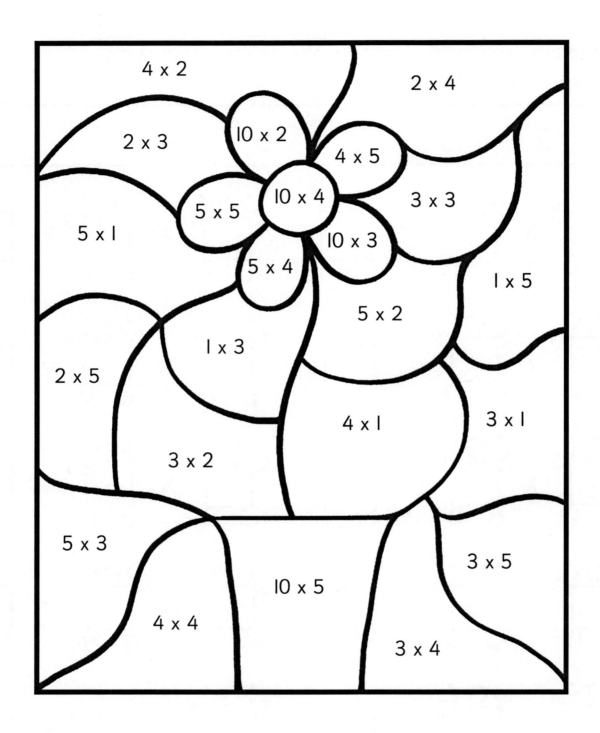

Colour the shapes blue if the answer is less than 11
green if the answer is from 11 to 19
yellow if the answer is from 20 to 30
red if the answer is more than 30.

Birds on the fence

Multiply the numbers on the fence by the numbers on the birds.

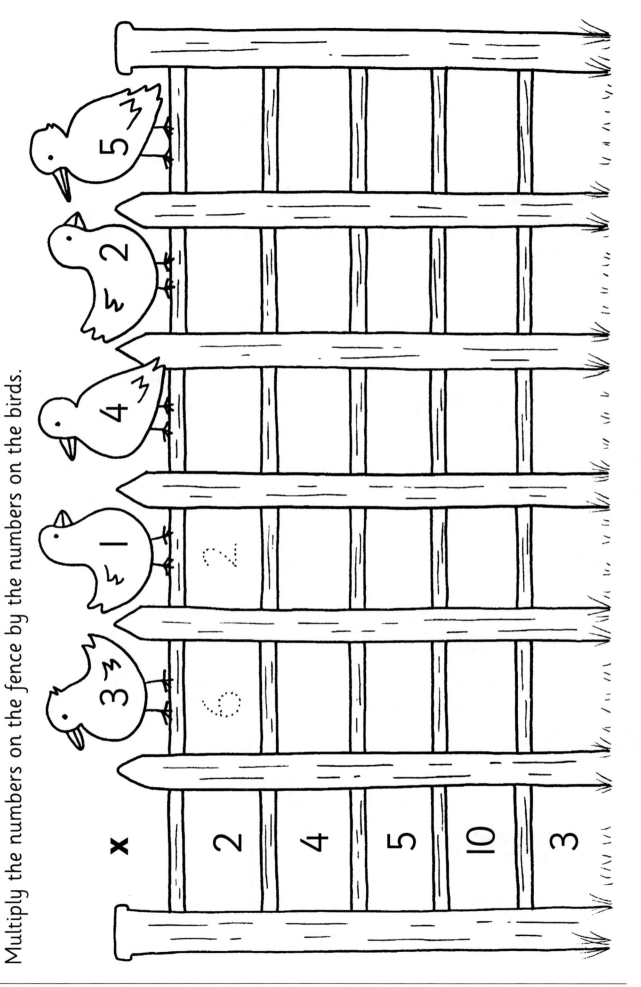

Where is my leaf?

Draw a line from each beetle to its leaf.

Snake sums

Colour the shapes red if the answer is 1
blue if the answer is 2
green if the answer is 3
yellow if the answer is 4
brown if the answer is 5.

Division function machines

Write the missing numbers on each machine.

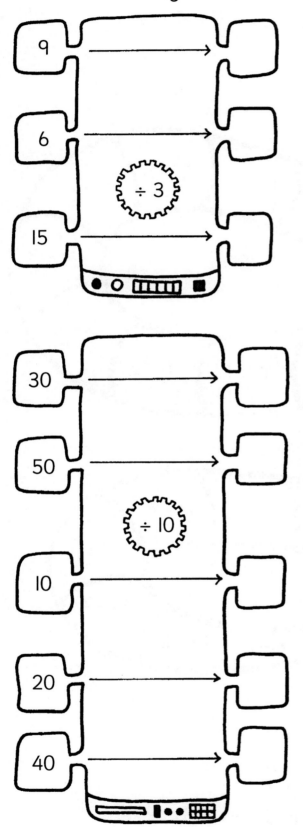

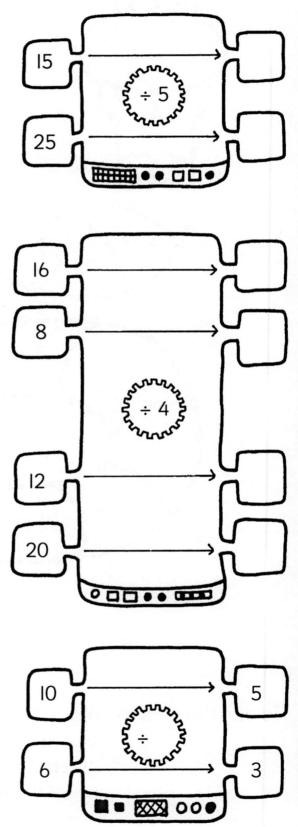

Frog jumps

Starting with the number on each frog's stone, take it on a journey, multiplying and dividing as you go. Write the numbers on the stones.

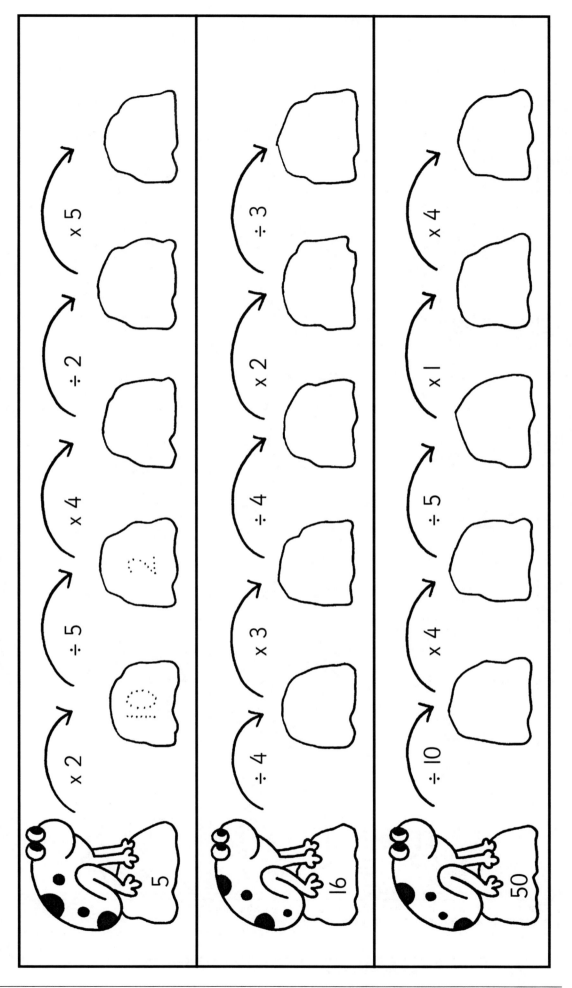

Penguin partners

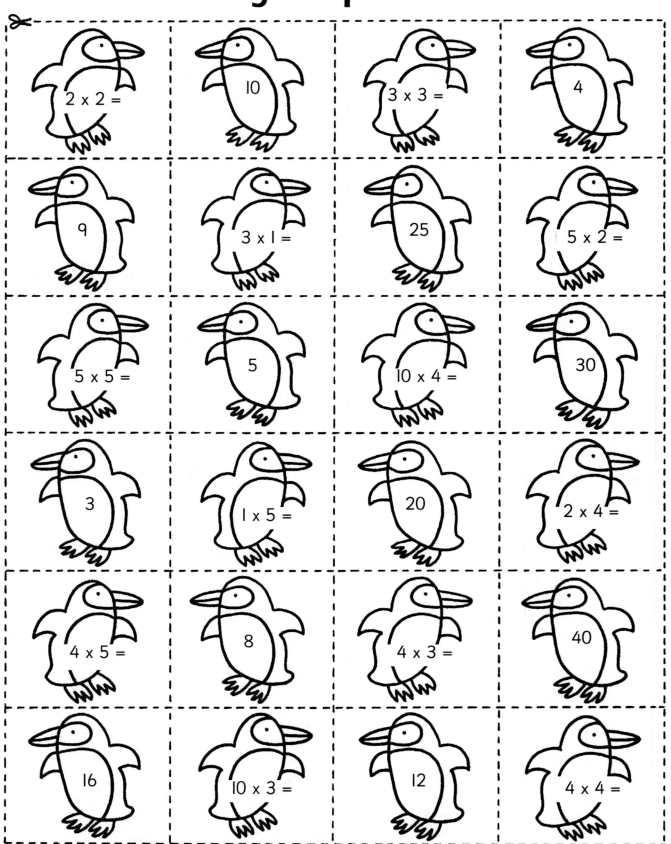

2 x 2 =	10	3 x 3 =	4
9	3 x 1 =	25	5 x 2 =
5 x 5 =	5	10 x 4 =	30
3	1 x 5 =	20	2 x 4 =
4 x 5 =	8	4 x 3 =	40
16	10 x 3 =	12	4 x 4 =

Game for 2 players, or alternatively, a matching activity for one child.
Equipment: 2 set rings and a calculator.
Stick the page on to card then cut along the dotted lines. Place the left-facing penguins face down in one set ring and the right-facing penguins in the other. The children take it in turns to choose 2 cards, one from each set ring. If the player thinks the cards match, he/she can keep them, but only after the other child has checked the answer on a calculator. The child with the most cards at the end of the game is the winner.

The kite game

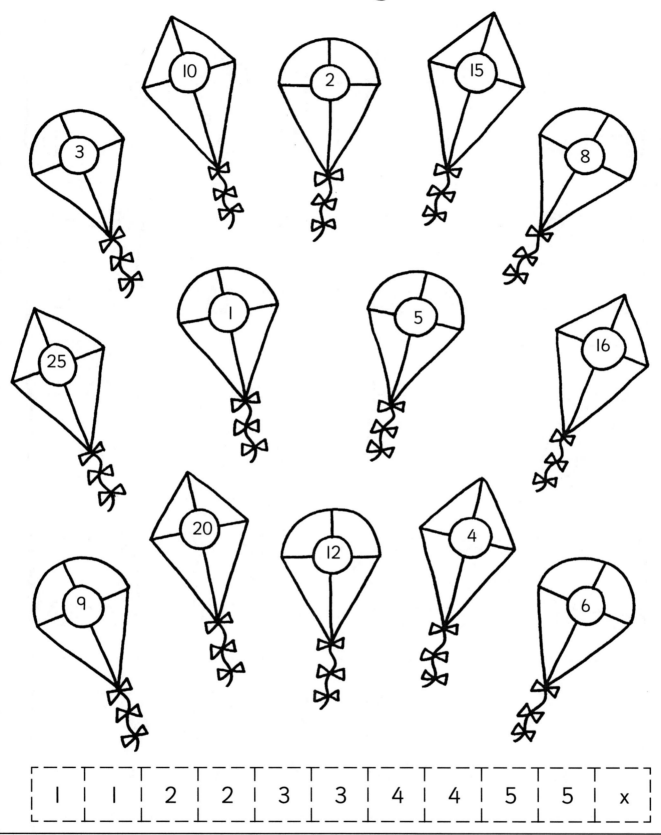

| I | I | I | 2 | 2 | 3 | 3 | 4 | 4 | 5 | 5 | x |

Game for 2 players.

Equipment: 2 different coloured crayons and a calculator.

Stick the numbers at the bottom on to card and cut along the dotted lines. Spread out the numbers face down on a surface. The children take it in turns to choose 2 numbers and multiply them together, matching the answer to the correct kite. The other player checks the sum on a calculator. If correct, the kite can be coloured in. If the kite has already been coloured, or if the answer is incorrect, then play reverts to the other child. The child with the most kites at the end of the game is the winner.

How to Sparkle at Beginning Multiplication & Division

Piglet partners

Game for 2 players, or alternatively, a matching activity for one child.
Equipment: 2 set rings and a calculator.
Stick the page on to card then cut along the dotted lines. Place the left-facing piglets face down in one set ring and the right-facing piglets in the other. The children take it in turns to choose 2 cards, one from each set ring. If the player thinks the cards match, he/she can keep them, but only after the other child has checked the answer on a calculator. The child with the most cards at the end of the game is the winner.

Lightning Source UK Ltd.
Milton Keynes UK
UKOW032348051011

179790UK00001B/25/P

Lightning Source UK Ltd.
Milton Keynes UK
UKOW07f180612061б
276085UK0003B/69/P